Tame the

Tame the Turbulence

Avoid Losing It.
Fly Through It.

10 Maneuvers to STOP Stress
from Spiraling Out of Control

Tracy Butz

TRACY BUTZ

Tame the Turbulence

Avoid Losing It.
Fly Through It.

Tracy Butz

Copyright © 2012 by Tracy Butz

Published by:
Lakeview Press
Menasha, Wisconsin

Lakeview
Press

Printed in the United States of America

Cover design by Mike Heidl
Edited by Tani Grimh

Library of Congress Control Number: 2012915260
ISBN: 978-0-9840061-8-2

Praise for
Tame the Turbulence

"This fast-moving book is loaded with great ideas and suggestions to help you get complete control of your life."

Brian Tracy, Legendary International Speaker and Bestselling Author

"Oh, how often we long for some practical wisdom that really is both doable and life-changing!! You are holding in your hands an amazing collection of transformational answers to your daily dilemmas! Dive in now. You will be so glad you did!"

Glenna Salsbury, Author of *The Art of The Fresh Start*

"Feeling like life is beating you up? Take time to *Tame the Turbulence* and get a dose of motivation. Tracy Butz uses her personal stories to set up life lessons that we can all learn from. Recommended dosage: One chapter daily."

Shep Hyken, *New York Times* Bestselling Business Author of *The Amazement Revolution*

"Wow! Another fabulous and delightful book by Tracy Butz! Tracy's personal stories inspire courage, confidence, and self-respect to help ease us through life's ups and downs, jolts and shakes. You'll feel more grounded with each page you turn!"

Emily Huling, President of Selling Strategies, Inc. and Author of *Kick Your "Butt"* and *Great Service Sells*

"*Tame the Turbulence,* with its real-life tips on managing stress, will help you make sure that your attitude is in its full, locked and upright position."

Karyn Ruth White, Motivational Keynote Comedian

"Coming from a perfectionist who has been through a lot of stress in my lifetime, I found that Tracy's new book captured many of the lessons that I had to learn the hard way over the last thirty years. Tracy's challenging life experiences have inspired her to pay her knowledge forward to help others learn from her without having to spend as much time, effort and frustration as I did on learning the same thing. Her real life stories are exciting, interesting and relevant to the topics at hand. I would recommend her book to everyone, unless you know someone without any stress in their life—good luck with that!"

Jeanne Rahr, Vice President Finance, Fosber America, Inc.

"When stress enters your life it can wreak havoc. This book will give you tools and techniques to get you through stress, while making you laugh and smile. Tracy's stories come from the heart and will help you make the connections between your health, stress, and letting it go."

Jill Stache, VP Commercial Lines Underwriting, Integrity Insurance

"I thoroughly enjoyed reading Tracy's very practical and insightful ideas contained in *Tame the Turbulence*. I have known Tracy for several years and have always marveled at how she could personally handle so many things at any one time, with an ease and grace that I don't think most of us could pull off. I am so glad that she has decided to let us all take a peek behind the veil to learn the strategies that may allow me to learn to do what I have seen her do firsthand. I would recommend her new book for anyone that wants to lessen the stress in their life."

Jeff Jenkins, Blueprint Consulting Group

"Tracy offers some great tips to help reduce the stress in your life. This is a must-read for those busy, working moms and dads who are constantly striving for perfection and enduring lots of stress to keep their family happy!"

Heather Resop, Corporate Trainer

Dedication

T his book is dedicated to those special individuals who continue to love, inspire and support me in my life.

To my loving husband and best friend, Kirt, a truly charismatic man who I laugh with and cherish life alongside every day.

To my wonderful young men, Taylor, Connor and Truman, who I love dearly and continue to be very proud of, with amazing futures in front of them.

Thank you for making life exciting, meaningful and fun!

Table of Contents

Introduction

Take a glass, fill it with marbles, and shake. That's what it can feel like inside an airplane hit by turbulence.

Turbulence can occur at any time on a flight, like when an aircraft passes over an unstable air mass and experiences rapidly rising or descending air.

Planes are designed to withstand the pressure of the atmosphere in flight, yet when severe turbulence hits, the sequence of events that follows can be absolutely terrifying. From tossing people from their seats and slamming them into the ceiling to loose galley items fiercely hurling around, intense panic among rattled passengers can be expected. Even though most turbulence is not severe, I would much rather avoid experiencing it all together.

Another type of turbulence, that has nothing to do with flying but is quite common today, is stress. Stress is a perceived threat to our mind, body, spirit or emotions, whereby the threat can be real or imagined. When people perceive something about a specific circumstance, they place their own interpretations on it. This is why two people in the exact same situation may respond differently. Stress, then, forms from combining the stressor and the body's reaction to it. Stressors are the triggers that cause us to experience stress. They can be major life events or small daily hassles. Temporary events, such as sudden danger, can cause stress, which is usually considered acute stress because, while intense, the duration is rather short. However, when stress lasts for a significant period of time, it is referred to as chronic stress.

Stress can be either positive or negative. Positive stress, known as eustress, can give us an extra burst of adrenaline to help us accomplish goals and meet deadlines, providing us with enhanced mental alertness, motivation, and even increased efficiency. Negative stress, called distress, generally occurs when your body can't return to a relaxed state even in the absence of the stessor. When negative stress accumulates—whether it's at work, at home, or anywhere— it can have extremely harmful effects on us, including issues like hypertension, a suppressed immune system, and chronic pain, just to name a few. Consequently, stress is considered by many experts to be the number one health problem today.

But is this health issue one we can mitigate or control? Let's consider experienced pilots for a moment, and what they do when they hit turbulence. Can we employ a pilot's approach to *tame the turbulence* in our daily lives?

Pilots avoid most turbulent air by studying weather reports and information received from other airplanes via the air traffic controller. However, if turbulence appears suddenly, pilots often are able to escape it by climbing to higher altitudes where the air is less rough. So pilots do what they can to avoid turbulence, yet they're prepared to apply specific maneuvers when they need to fly through it.

As we yearn for the ability to live more productive, balanced and meaningful lives, I suggest we follow the same methodology as pilots. When encountering negative stress in our daily lives, stay calm, take control, and *Tame the Turbulence* by applying the 10 Maneuvers outlined in this book. Simply put...*Avoid losing it. Fly through it.*

Chapter 1

Undress Your Stress

"Stress is an important dragon to slay—or at least tame—in your life." **Marilu Henner**

"For every minute you are angry, you lose sixty seconds of happiness." **Unknown**

"The greatest weapon against stress is our ability to choose one thought over another." **William James**

Tame the Turbulence

Undress Your Stress

It was December 2008 and my husband, Kirt, and I were on vacation in Cabo San Lucas, Mexico, pampering ourselves at a luxurious resort with a breathtaking ocean-side view. On the beach, we took it all in, feeling the hot sand beneath our feet and between our toes; the calm, cool and salty waves gently caressing our bodies; and the powerful luminous rays warming our skin. From a relaxing poolside massage under a cabana, to a romantic evening voyage aboard a catamaran, to the delectable authentic cuisine we enjoyed each evening near the town square, this truly was an exquisite escape that exceeded all expectations...except for one memorable adventure we dove into near the end of our trip.

We thought it would be fun to take a scuba-diving excursion together. Kirt dove twice before but still joined me in a beginner's course, as I was new to this rather intimidating sport. The three-hour course promised comprehensive instruction for someone who has never scuba-dove, plus a thirty-minute dive along the ocean floor. Lucky for us, we were the only two registered for that timeslot and were thrilled to have the instructor's undivided attention.

Our instructor was highly charismatic, very friendly, and obviously well-known at this dive shop, which was somewhat comforting. He began the instruction, though, with a style I quickly became concerned with because of being quite familiar with training best practices. While still on land, he conceptually taught us how to breathe in the water and how to equalize any pressure we may feel. He then demonstrated an emergency signal to use in the event we had an issue with something like getting adequate airflow.

Before we knew it, fifteen to twenty minutes elapsed and our instructor said, "Let's go into the shop and get on our gear." I was delighted to hear him say this, as I was anxious to practice what we had just learned in a few feet of water. To my horror and disbelief, we were escorted aboard a small boat with another group and quickly ventured into fairly high, choppy ocean waves. As the boat rocked vigorously, water now spilling over the sides of our undersized craft, a small part of me still felt reassured that I would receive more one-on-one direction once we reached our destination. I couldn't have been more wrong.

The anchor dropped and the instructor said, "We need to be really careful. The current is super strong today." He handed me two fins, and as I put them on, I realized they were different sizes, the larger barely staying on my foot standing in the boat. After bringing the issue to his attention, he lackadaisically replied, "No worries, it'll be just fine," as he finished tying an incredibly heavy weight around my waist so that once in the water, I wouldn't buoy to the top. My heart started beating fast with trepidation when I realized my air tank wasn't working properly. "Okay, there we go. It's working now," he declared a few moments later. My hubby turned to me for the third time and softly offered me a way out saying, "It is absolutely fine for you to stay on the boat; I have no problem diving alone. I can tell you are really nervous and I don't blame you for feeling that way. This is not even close to how I learned to dive."

I am definitely not an adventurous individual, yet I so badly wanted to share this special experience with my husband, so I remained committed.

Have you ever been in a situation where your sixth sense is screaming at you, yet you chose to ignore the warning?

Kirt went first, diving backward into the high waves. He was instructed to begin getting used to his equipment and to practice breathing under the water. As I drummed up the courage and positioned myself to enter the water, the instructor said he would follow me shortly and to just hang tight in the water.

Upon entering the cold water near the front of the boat, the current was even more tumultuous than it appeared, and my feet immediately were swept under the boat. I clenched onto a rope attached to the side of the vessel, frantically trying to maintain my grip, keep my head above water, and keep that one loose and useless fin on my foot. Spotting the instructor entering the water, I also could see that Kirt was quite a distance from me. He was trying to maneuver his way over to me as quickly as he could, yet with his heavy equipment and the strong current, he was struggling. I began to panic even more, frantically looking around for help—with eyes as big as the body of a stressed out pufferfish—while repeatedly struggling to scream and taking in salty water with each short yelp.

The instructor made it to me first, grabbed ahold of me, and towed me to the backside of the vessel where the current was not as robust. With my body returned to an appropriate vertical position, I tried to catch my breath and calm my nerves, while exhaustively declaring, "I need to be done." Undoubtedly disturbed by my lack of sustain, the instructor said in an unapologetic and abrasive tone, "You can do what you want, but this is a once-in-a-lifetime experience that you'll be giving up, and you won't get your money back!"

Stunned by his un-empathetic and disparaging nature, I began to challenge my fears. My husband, finally able to push through the powerful current, was relieved to find me clearly shaken, yet physically okay. Feeling determined to override my anxiety, I wasn't going to let fear take control and stand in the way of this experience—for me or us. I consciously decided to continue, saying cautiously, "I guess I will give it one more try."

As we slowly dropped 40 feet locked arm-in-arm, Kirt and I saw some beautiful coral formations, vibrant fish, and other interesting ocean life. I can honestly say that I was able to appreciate the last ten minutes of the thirty-minute dive. Interestingly, as soon as I was able to balance the stress I was feeling and reacting to—physically, mentally, and emotionally—I began to relax a bit and appreciate the experience. Maybe I wasn't actually enjoying myself, but by persevering, I was able to experience an excursion I never thought I would attempt.

Stress in everyday life is similar, giving us moments of fear and doubt, a tremendous adrenaline rush, and sometimes all of those feelings combined. See, stress can be positive, keeping us alert and ready to avoid danger; or negative, bringing on or worsening numerous symptoms and diseases, potentially causing adverse health effects, such as headaches, sleep disturbances, feelings of anxiety or tension, anger, concentration problems, depression, a lack of interest in food or an increased appetite, or even absolute burnout. So this stress stuff shouldn't be taken lightly.

The great news, is there are 10 Maneuvers outlined in this book that can be applied immediately to help stop stress from spiraling out of control. The first step: *undress your stress*. By understanding the sources of stress you experience and to be cognizant of various signs and symptoms before stress hits, you will be able to more effectively manage stress in your life.

So what are sources of stress in your life? Does it involve your job, kids, strained relationships, being overcommitted, financial obligations, health concerns, something entirely different, or all of the above? If you don't know, take some time to expose what those are, but know it isn't as easy to uncover as it sounds. Your true sources of stress aren't always obvious, and it's all too easy to overlook your own stress-inducing thoughts, feelings, and behaviors. Sure, you may know that you're often worried about work deadlines, but maybe it's your procrastination, rather than the actual job demands, that leads to your stress about tight targets.

To identify your true sources of stress, look closely at your habits, attitude, and maybe even excuses that slip out:

- Do you explain away stress as a temporary condition, yet can't remember the last time you put your feet up? An example may sound similar to this: "I just have a million things going on right now!"
- Do you define stress as an integral part of your work or home life or as part of your personality? I hear people voice this rationale by saying things like: "It's always crazy around here," or "I have a lot of nervous energy today."
- Do you blame your stress on other people or outside events, or view it as entirely normal? If so, it may sound something like, "They always make me feel that way," or "That's just the way this time of year is for me."

Once you realize the origin of your turbulence and what is being hidden underneath it, pay attention to the warning signs and symptoms you see and feel. What are they for you?

Have you become less decisive, more irritable, have a short temper, bite your nails, pace back and forth, grind your teeth, pick fights, have racing thoughts, display poor judgment, have bouts of insomnia, feel increased muscle tension, or deal with undeniable fatigue? This is obviously a very short list of things to be aware of. But once you realize what they are for you, you can begin to address your stress, to help *tame the turbulence* in your life. Learn how to stop stress from spiraling out of control. Instead, recognize the symptoms, make an adjustment, and then continue with a revised, instead of wrecked, flight plan.

Chapter 2

Lighten the Load

"Don't be shy about asking for help. It doesn't mean you're weak, it only means you're wise." **Unknown**

"There is more to life than increasing its speed." **Mohandas K. Gandhi**

"Procrastination is the thief of time." **Edward Young**

Tame the Turbulence

Lighten the Load

You, like me, are probably being asked to do more today than you did a year ago. Whether it is at work or at home, the tasks continue to come. And even though we sometimes feel we're the only ones capable of doing something, it's usually not the case—adding to our current level of stress.

Sometimes it's easier for us to allow ourselves to feel overwhelmed rather than ask for help. However, taking care of the household, children, parents, errands, appointments, and pets doesn't need to be the responsibility of just one person. There are many things that we can do to decrease the number of tasks we're responsible for, and in the process, become generally happier, more pleasant, and helpful to others, like our families, friends, and colleagues. Heck, we may even like ourselves a little more, too, because we won't see that scowling face staring back at us each day.

As you consider ways to *tame the turbulence* in your life, the second key maneuver is to *lighten the load*. Following are some strategies to get started.

When examining our list of to-dos, it is important to realize that not all tasks are created equal. And if you don't prioritize them, someone else usually will. So, if you want to *lighten your load*, one critical strategy is to take charge of your time. Reclaiming control of your time starts with thinking through all of the tasks that are on your mind and transferring them from your head to paper. As you create this long list, ensure you separate out what truly *needs* to get done versus what you would *like* to get done, noting the dates that they are to be completed by.

From the "need to" list, prioritize all of the tasks in order of importance, also noting the amount of time you believe it will take to complete each one. By seeing what you *need* to do, you can determine if accomplishing the list is even plausible. If it appears attainable, you now have a detailed plan you can work through. However, if the list looks unreasonable, it's time to make some adjustments.

One change you could consider is to scan the "need to" tasks to see if any of them should be moved over to the "want to" column. Another tweak could be revising the completion date, especially for tasks that don't involve another person counting on you to complete your part before he/she can proceed. A third modification that may be helpful is to review tasks that may no longer need to be accomplished—contemplate what items you may be able to stop doing and cross them off the list. For example, maybe you have been responsible for a report that you have printed and distributed monthly to your team for several years. Determine if that report is still needed and used. If not, that is one task that can be crossed off your list immediately. However, if that report is still necessary, see if the frequency of the report can be modified (from monthly to quarterly) or if it could be accessed online instead. Either way, you will have opened up some time on your calendar, which is something we all would love.

Regardless of how many tasks we have, until they are written down with completion dates, the expected time needed to do the tasks, and if they are things we really need to accomplish, it is difficult to understand the situation we are facing. We are likely really stressing more about the unknown than about the task list itself.

Once you've prioritized and correctly categorized your to-do list, strategy number two under *lighten the load* is to ask for help. Unless you have a large red "S" on your chest, you likely don't have super powers, which may be what it would take for one individual to conquer this evil list. Ask your spouse, partner, roommate or other family members to help. This includes children who live with you, whether they are 4 or 40. Remember, people often don't mind helping. In fact, they usually don't realize you need help, and in many cases, loved ones want to help but they simply don't know how. I have found that when I ask for help from a family member or colleague, the overwhelming feeling associated with the tasks decreases immediately. It also provides others with a sense of contribution—helping address the needs of your family or work team.

Let's use laundry as an example. Why should one person have to do all the laundry for the entire family? The answer I hear from people I talk with usually is, "Because that's how it's always been." Fortunately, for many of us, it doesn't have to be this way. Choose to *lighten the load* for you by asking others for some help. It doesn't make you weak or incapable. Asking for help makes you *wise*. We cannot continue to do more and more, no matter how much we want to or feel we should be able to. Sooner or later, we will face turbulence so strong that we'll end up crashing. Look over that list, whether it is at home or work, and consider each task along with each of your family members or colleagues that you are thinking about requesting help from. Determine who may best be able to assist with each task based on age, skill, length of task, other current responsibilities, etc.

Generally speaking, most people feel a strong sense of connection when asked to help someone in need. However, for those who tend to whine a bit when asked to do something extra, it may be helpful to consider if we are enabling these individuals somewhat—meaning that, because we avoid asking these people for assistance due to the anticipated backlash, we allow them a free seat on the plane. This really isn't how it is supposed to work. Helping one another feels good. Really good, in fact. For what is perceived as small and doable to one, can be large and daunting to another, especially to those who are close to losing it. Asking for help is not only smart, it helps others feel good too.

After you have prioritized your tasks, asked for help from others, and maybe even considered hiring a professional service or two to complete some of the more arduous tasks, a third strategy to *lighten the load* is to cut back on planned activities for both you and your family.

When my boys were young, we planned out in advance fun things to do over the summer. As crazy as this may sound, my family had numerous "fun" activities assigned to every weekend, which for one weekend literally may include: Visit a nearby zoo, enjoy rides and games at a county fair, watch an exciting movie at a local theatre, splash around at a public pool, cheer on my son at his baseball game, and go out to dinner with friends. This was all on top of going grocery shopping, running kids here and there, doing chores around the house, writing out bills, picking up more groceries because my hungry boys never stop eating, fixing broken stuff around the house, doing the fifth load of laundry, mowing the lawn, and then choosing to go to the nearby gas station and pay double for milk, because we ran out and going back to the grocery store for the third time in two days was where we drew the line.

I realize the activities may sound fun, but looking at this list as an older and wiser woman, I suggest you learn a key life lesson far earlier than I did: By doing less, you get more.

Squeezing additional activities into an already jam-packed schedule may result in doing more stuff, but it also usually leads to more stress. Even though you are attempting to have more fun, doing more is actually providing less of a quality experience. Instead, I recommend picking one activity that you feel your family and/or friends would enjoy. The planning, anticipation and energy around this one activity will be much more positive, allowing you to truly enjoy the moment as it unfolds. You won't have to worry about when you need to leave to get to the next thing. You'll tend to be more playful, relaxed, and able to take in the experience to a higher degree. You'll have the flexibility to stay longer if you're having fun and add some spontaneity, if desired. Choose quality over quantity, and watch your experiences become far more meaningful and fulfilling.

The fourth strategy I find helpful when aspiring to *lighten the load*, is to know it's not only okay, but highly recommended, to slow down the process of saying yes and even consider a no once in a while. Now, if you have a difficult time saying no on the spot, know that you are not alone. Know, too, there are other ways to respond besides answering with a direct yes or no. If you're uncomfortable, say you will think it over and let that person know in the next day or so. Then when you follow up, you could use one of these helpful techniques:

- Describe what you could do instead (modification of what was asked).
- Clarify that it can be done, but in order to do a quality job, you will need additional time (be specific as to how much time).

- Explain how you have other commitments that you need to follow through on first to maintain your integrity with what you have already promised.
- If you know of another person who would enjoy this challenge, consider recommending him/her for the task. Be careful not to suggest someone who also has a full plate. I usually check with the person before recommending him/her.

The next time someone comes to you with a task that has a deadline you know you can't make or will push back another one you've already committed to, realize there are options. Instead of feeling stuck, feel empowered by knowing you have a workable maneuver to help you gain altitude and pull out of the turbulence you feel.

A fifth strategy to *lighten the load* is to stop spending time to save money. Stop throwing away your precious time traveling all the way across town just for a fantastic deal on one item. I know most of us have done this...at least once! The money you save gets chewed up in the time you spend. What is your time worth? Is driving and standing in line worth one hour of your time? Instead, group errands, tackling them one right after the other, saving both time and money. For example, if you are planning to go to the grocery store for two items, to the bank to cash a check, to a department store for a lengthy list of things, and to the gas station to fuel up, combine all of those errands into one trip, ensuring you think through the route before leaving home.

Avoid going to the grocery store for just two items and pick up those essentials from the department store.

Also incorporated into strategy five that helps us to avoid spending time to save a few bucks, is to look at *when* you run errands. If you work a fairly traditional Monday through Friday schedule, it is best to avoid venturing out on weekends, if possible. Weekends are when most people run their errands, which consumes more of your valuable time than necessary waiting in check-out lines and heavy traffic. Maybe you could head out one evening, right after you ask a family member to help clean up dinner. Or, if weekday evenings are out of the question, could you consider running out before work or during lunch? By altering the day and/or time you run errands, you can lessen the burden, especially when you are second in line versus thirteenth. Rather than running and waiting, and then waiting some more, choose to free up that precious weekend time to do other things that are far more fun—like those things that are written on your "want to" list.

Now you have five key strategies designed to help you *lighten your load*. The amazing aspect about this maneuver is that you will see immediate benefit. You'll gain five minutes here, fifteen minutes there, and before you know it, you will have carved out an extra hour to do whatever you want. You could spend this precious time hanging out with friends, taking your pet for a walk, watching a movie with your spouse, or simply enjoying it all yourself.

Chapter 3

Forget Perfect

"The best things in life are yours if you can appreciate yourself." **Dale Carnegie**

"Strive for progress, not perfection." **Unknown**

"Excellence is to do a common thing in an uncommon way." **Booker T. Washington**

Tame the Turbulence

Forget Perfect

In theory, striving for perfection should foster success and happiness. In reality, it rarely does. More often than not, perfectionism impedes success. For some, the desire to *be* perfect, or *become* perfect, or *appear* perfect, arises from a mistaken belief that super-high achievement is the best or only route to exemplify a successful life. For others, perfectionism results from a desire to win social approval by impressing others, avoiding criticism, or not being seen making mistakes.

Whatever its source and whatever its form, perfection is impossible. No matter how you define it, there's something you could change to make whatever *it* is even better. There is no perfect—no one is, and no one should expect you to be. *Forget Perfect* is the third maneuver to help *tame the turbulence* in your life.

But, as many know, the pursuit of perfection rarely disappears from the radar without a strong, committed effort.

A *perfect* example of pursuing perfection comes from the summer before entering high school. I was exceedingly driven and self-disciplined in most aspects of my life. Pushing beyond what I thought I could do was a challenge I found exhilarating. Amazingly, I made the high school Pom Pom Squad as the second sophomore ever to be awarded the honor. It was thrilling, yet I had a new summer job working close to fulltime, and a boyfriend whom I adored. My perfectionism was steadily progressing, seeking to be the best athlete, the hardest worker, and the most admired girlfriend, with a slim, muscular physique envied by all, despite being the result of unhealthy eating habits and an excessive exercise regime.

One morning I woke to three small BB-sized bumps on my chest, with it quickly spreading within a couple of days like a massive, uncontrolled wildfire. My mother, very concerned, quickly took me to the doctor.

I learned I had shingles, a viral infection that causes an extremely painful rash, usually found in the elderly, rarely attacking teenagers. I was told it likely was caused from not enough sleep, a lack of nutrition, and too much stress. That clearly described my lifestyle. I ended up with one of the worst cases my physician had ever seen, with the oozing, burning sores extending from my right upper back, over my shoulder, along the entire right side of my neck, down and over to the middle of my chest, causing significant nerve inflammation beneath the skin. I spent two weeks essentially in bed, getting up only when absolutely necessary. The pain was so excruciating in my right arm that I couldn't even move it. My daily routine consisted of choking down twelve pills and eating what I was able to in bed, with my mom carefully applying liquid soap to my open sores to help them heal. Most of my days and nights were spent sleeping and trying to fight it.

Because of this experience, I do clearly recall significant changes I needed to make in my life. Gone were the days of carelessness and self-neglect. I needed to learn how to manage my life better and lower my level of stress, which meant I needed to let go of perfectionism.

So what does it take? How can we free ourselves and *forget perfect*? Here are some suggestions I find helpful:

- **Abandon the pretense of "perfectability."** None of us are perfect and no one ever will be—which is great, because we can simply stop pretending it's possible.
- **Heighten awareness to your thoughts and actions.** Notice when perfectionism is pulling at you before reacting negatively.
- **Learn to prioritize and focus.** Doing so will allow you to be excellent at what's important and good enough at everything else.
- **Set your own goals—realistic ones.** Look at your life and the direction you want it to take. Set goals that you want to achieve and realistically know you can attain with a fair amount of dedicated effort. Be careful that your goals aren't too easy; challenge creates the desire to stretch yourself, feeling a greater sense of pride when you accomplish what you set out to do.

- **Consider effort over outcome.** Realize the success you've achieved based on effort, which is within your control, versus outcome, which is often influenced by external factors and outside of your control.
- **Treat feedback as a gift.** When you are offered or given feedback, whether it is positive or constructive, listen attentively and take it for what it is— information that someone chose to share with you for some reason. Instead of dwelling on or worrying about it, validate the feedback with another person if necessary, and then choose either to make a change or let it go. Gaining another perspective, especially when the person's intent is genuine, can provide valuable guidance and direction.
- **View mistakes as necessary steps on the path to improvement—not as flaws.** With each step you take, continue to get better. Learn from what didn't work, and get that much closer to your goal.

Perfection is a fallacy of irrational thinking—the more we try to be perfect, the more disappointed we will be. Rather than shooting for perfection, aim for your finest, and you will rarely let yourself down. Put the abundance of time and effort into delivering your best, letting the misfires fall where they may. Instead, look in the mirror, and see a reflection glowing with an abundance of pride.

Chapter 4

Treat the Disease to Please

"Good decisions come from experience, and experience comes from bad decisions." **Unknown**

"We tend to forget that happiness doesn't come as a result of getting something we don't have, but rather of recognizing and appreciating what we do have." **Frederick Keonig**

"Your time is limited, so don't waste it living someone else's life." **Steve Jobs**

Tame the Turbulence

Treat the Disease
to Please

O ne common companion to trying to be perfect and trying to do too much is trying to please everyone. Are you overly concerned with impressing, winning the approval of, or incessantly pleasing someone? Needing to please other people, no matter what the personal cost to you, is a symptom of the *disease to please*. By defining healthier boundaries, you can treat this disease and *tame the turbulence* it brings.

Personal boundaries, the space around you that gives you a clear sense of who you are and where you're going, are triggered when you choose to allow someone or something into it. For example, if my son asks for yet *another* ride to his buddy's house and I can't say no without feeling guilty, then I'm probably not protecting my personal boundaries. If your colleague consistently expects you to help him do part of his work and you haven't figured out how to say no, then you are allowing someone else to control some of your personal boundaries.

For many, the difficulty may start innocently enough with genuine and generous attempts to make others happy. But this seemingly harmless passion to be nice, to put others first, and to please others even at the expense of one's own health and happiness, can spiral into some far-reaching physical and emotional consequences.

Personal boundaries can become weak or essentially nonexistent, which is often referred to as being the proverbial "doormat." I have seen this happen to friends and colleagues, through small, repeated doses of self-doubt, feeling overly vulnerable, being unclear about their feelings and what they want and need, and/or struggling with loneliness, distrust, anger or control. Those who continue to struggle with pleasing others often say yes to most requests, because they may fear rejection, inherently will do anything they can to avoid conflict, and tend to tolerate disrespectful treatment because they feel it may be justified in some way. To put this all in simple terms, life doesn't have to be this way and everyone deserves more than that. Remember: nobody can make you feel inferior unless you give him or her permission.

In one of my first real romantic relationships, I found myself open to doing a lot of new and exciting things, and many well outside my comfort zone. For example, I had never been snow skiing before, but I tried it, and was literally petrified from learning how to "snow plow" on a miniscule beginner's bunny hill to unknowingly transitioning to a dangerous black diamond hill. Ironically, this became the sport-of-choice for *us*, even though being out in the cold weather was not something I looked forward to. I even agreed to spend an entire month over winter break working at a ski hill. Why, you ask? The answer didn't come to me until years later, when I had a tough time admitting how my life had evolved into something I barely recognized as my own. I felt alone and suffocated, as if I was trying to make a change, yet wasn't strong enough to do it. I wasn't living *my* life, aligned with my needs, desires and goals. I was living life for someone else.

Have you ever felt similar emotions or do you know someone who is struggling with a comparable situation?

Here are some signs of unhealthy boundary issues to watch for and treat, if needed:

- Going against personal values to please others.
- Letting others define you.
- Expecting others to fill your needs automatically.
- Feeling bad or guilty when you say no.
- Not speaking up when you are treated poorly.
- Falling apart so someone can take care of you.
- Falling in love with someone you barely know or who reaches out to you.
- Accepting advances or intimacy that you don't want.

How can we pursue and set healthy boundaries, where we live the life we want to live, rather than existing in another person's shadow? I believe it starts by knowing what you like, need, want, and don't want, and then making choices which are aligned with those needs and wants. That doesn't mean you live your life without compromise or flexibility; you just don't give into the demands and unrealistic expectations of others. Following are some thoughts and actions that lead to healthier boundaries:

- **Develop a strong sense of personal identity.** Realize and take pride in what makes you unique.
- **Respect yourself.** Feel an inner confidence and assurance, *independent of praise from others*.
- **Be respectful of others.** Look for positive and honorable qualities in others.
- **Forgive.** Forgive others and yourself. Move on from past mistakes and difficult situations.
- **Accept accountability.** When things go wrong, be accountable for your mistakes without pointing fingers at others.
- **Teach your lips to say no.** Understand that you are free to say yes or no. And, when appropriate, you should do so without feelings of guilt, anger or fear.
- **Expect mutual benefit in relationships.** Whether at work or at home, healthy relationships should provide value and benefit for both parties. It likely won't be the same for each of you, but it should be a shared venture.
- **Welcome feedback.** Some feedback is positive, and some is constructive. Understand the intent of the other person, and try to look past how it was delivered. Choose to learn and grow from feedback you receive.

- **Refuse to take on the problems of others.** It is admirable to help others through difficult situations; however, there is a big difference between offering assistance and accepting another person's problem as your own.
- **Celebrate successes.** Celebrate personal accomplishments by treating yourself to a movie, taking a vacation day to do what *you* want, indulging in a small treat, etc. Additionally, get in the habit of noticing and applauding the success of others. By recognizing another person's achievements, you are demonstrating value and appreciation for their effort and results.

I realize that *treating the disease to please* and making brave choices in the process isn't easy. Putting your needs first and teaching others how to treat us can be very difficult. Actually admitting how you feel to yourself may be one of the hardest things you'll ever do. Yet I have found that after feeling a little guilty at first, you likely will have less turbulence in your life—eventually feeling and being much happier, more liberated, less stressed, and a lot stronger. You will be a better *you*.

Chapter 5

Sleep Baby Sleep

"If you can't sleep, then get up and do something instead of lying there worrying. It's the worry that gets you, not the lack of sleep." **Dale Carnegie**

"The time to relax is when you don't have time for it." **Jim Goodwin**

"People who say they sleep like a baby usually don't have one." **Leo J. Burke**

Tame the Turbulence

Sleep Baby Sleep

Everywhere we look there are ads that suggest if we take this or do that, we will have found the secret to more vitality and zest for life. But I don't believe in magic pills or miracle ointments. Instead, I have one solution that has helped me in all facets of my life: Sleep.

Interestingly, there are competing beliefs about how much sleep we need. Is it six hours? Seven hours? Eight hours? Is there an optimum amount of sleep necessary for a healthy adult? I don't think so. In fact, I believe it really depends on the individual and his/her lifestyle and needs.

Eight hours of sleep for many adults seems like a luxury, although, that is actually not enough sleep for me. My body and mind need nine or ten hours of quality sleep to feel rejuvenated, energized and poised to stand tall—even though I measure just shy of 5'3". I realize you may wonder how it is possible to get that much sleep. For me, the choice is simple.

In 1997, I was diagnosed with Systemic Lupus, an auto-immune disease that thankfully I have been able to keep in remission for the past 11 years. I know getting enough quality sleep is critical for sustaining my good health, and I choose to make it a priority in my life.

So instead of considering how much sleep you can *get by with*, a much more productive and healthier question to ask is, "How much sleep do I *need*?"

If you want to *tame the turbulence* in your life, I highly recommend maneuver number four, *sleep baby sleep*. Why? Because getting enough z-z-z's is necessary for good health, specifically in these ways, according to the Division of Sleep Medicine at Harvard Medical School:

- **Learning and memory.** Sleep helps the brain commit new information to memory.
- **Metabolism and weight.** Sleep affects the way our bodies process and store carbohydrates, and alters levels of hormones that affect our appetite. Getting the right amount of sleep for your body will help you maintain a healthy weight.
- **Stress reduction.** A good night's sleep can help lower blood pressure and elevated levels of stress hormones, often brought on by a fast-paced lifestyle.
- **Safety.** Getting the right amount of sleep helps us to feel more alert and conscientious while we're awake. There is a decreased tendency to fall asleep when we need to be attentive, thus lowering the chances of making grave mistakes, such as medical errors, air traffic mishaps, and road accidents.

- **Mood.** Getting adequate sleep allows us to have the energy to do the things we like to do. It also stabilizes our mood, resulting in less irritability, impatience and concentration issues.
- **Cardiovascular health.** Quality sleep is known to provide significant benefits to our overall cardiovascular health, avoiding serious issues like hypertension, increased stress hormone levels, and irregular heartbeat.
- **Immune system.** Getting enough proper sleep strengthens the immune system and increases your ability to fight off chronic disease. Get the quality sleep you need and allow your body to stay strong, healthy and resilient.

Clearly, sleep offers many benefits for those of us wanting to live healthy lives. But there is one additional benefit that often flies under the radar. Do you want in on the secret? The huge hush-hush is something that can positively affect any adult, no matter your gender, ethnicity, height, weight, personality style, financial status, etc. Have you figured it out? The clandestine advantage that sleep provides is that it also defies the aging process. Securing "forty winks" is known to be an important time for the body's repair mechanisms to spring into action, producing growth hormones to help repair tissue damage. Who doesn't want to capitalize on looking younger and preventing wrinkles?

Now, many people I talk with say, "I realize sleep is important and that there are numerous benefits, but I have a tough time getting a good night's sleep." If you happen to have similar struggles getting enough quality shut-eye, you're not alone. According to the Center for Disease Control and Prevention, more than one-quarter of the U.S. population reports not getting enough sleep, while nearly 10 percent experience chronic insomnia. If you are one of those unfortunate individuals or know someone who struggles with sleep issues, here are twelve practical prescriptions to sleep better tonight:

Rx #1: Maintain a consistent sleep schedule. Start by getting to bed and getting up at the same time every day, including weekends. As tempting as it may be, don't try to make up for a lack of sleep by staying in bed on the weekends. Sleeping in won't make up for a sleep deficit. In fact, according to a recent Harvard study, when you snooze extra hours to compensate for sleep deprivation, your ability to focus is worse than if you had stayed up all night.

Rx #2: Create a comfy and cozy haven. Make your bedroom environment conducive to how you sleep best in terms of the amount of light, temperature of the room, and appropriate background noise. Plus, if you are able to crawl into a bed that is lined with super soft sheets, it often makes you feel like you are in a positive, comfortable and welcoming space, rather than one you want to jump out of.

Rx #3: If you nap, keep it short. According to the experts, naps can provide significant health benefits, like repairing a body at the cellular level, improving heart function, and providing a more balanced regulation of hormone levels.

Rx #4: Exercise by day to sleep at night. Engaging in regular exercise during the day can help you sleep better at night. However, you should avoid revving yourself up with high-intensity exercise near bedtime. If nighttime is when you are able to exercise, though, and that part of your schedule cannot be altered, choose a more relaxing type of exercise, like yoga versus running. As always, check with your doctor before starting an exercise regimen.

Rx #5: Wind down your brain. Shortly after dinner or at least two hours before heading to bed, take a little time to tie up loose ends from the day and plan out your next one. This way you can have time before bed to let go of anxieties and relax. However, even with your best efforts, clearing your mind before laying your head down for bed can be tough. If this happens, keep a pen and paper handy, within reach of your bed, so you can write down what is on your mind. Even though you are writing in the dark and your penmanship may not be the easiest to read in the morning, you likely will be able to understand the scribbles. More importantly, though, this strategy provides assurance that your concerns or tasks won't be forgotten and they can be addressed the next day.

Rx #6: Choose evening snacks wisely. When you want to snack in the evening, choose a healthy one, like a piece of fruit or low-fat crackers. Avoid foods that are spicy and contain a significant amount of oil, as they can trigger heartburn or an upset stomach.

Rx #7: Indulge in a bath. Before going to bed, try relaxing in a warm bubble bath. It's also helpful to add a few drops of aromatic lavender oil to the water, which has known calming effects. And yes, men can enjoy this, too!

Rx #8: Enjoy bedtime reading. Reading is another useful aid to falling asleep gently. Choose short stories or articles that don't require too much thinking or invoke high emotion.

Rx #9: Treat yourself to a massage. Every time I get a massage, my body feels like a wet noodle and all I want to do is slide into bed and say, "Lights out." If you have never tried a massage, I highly recommend it. A skilled masseuse will help your body relax and make the tension disappear.

Rx #10: Be mindful of actions day-to-day. Trying to sleep with feelings of guilt and regret are obviously not relaxing and may tend to keep your mind busily worrying and contriving. Instead, make good choices, aligned with your values, so you can maintain a healthy conscience.

Rx #11: Listen to soft music. For many of us, listening to soft, instrumental music has a relaxing effect, often helping us to fall asleep. Soothing music like this can be purchased from a local department store or downloaded individually from the internet to create your own calming collection.

Rx #12: Drink fluids as usual throughout the day, consuming less a few hours before bed. As bedtime draws closer, limit your fluid intake, so your sleep is not disrupted due to a full bladder. Common sense is not always common practice; therefore, it's worth mentioning.

As you seek to *tame the turbulence* in your life, look to sleep as a foundational and viable maneuver. Ignore those who say, "If you snooze, you lose," as that is a very unhealthy view. Realize all the health benefits that sleep provides, and give your body the sleep it needs rather than just the bare minimum. After all, consistently getting the right amount of quality sleep for *you* is "just what the doctor ordered."

Chapter 6

Workout Your Worry

"Those who think they have not time for bodily exercise will sooner or later have to find time for illness." **Edward Stanley**

"Strength does not come from physical capacity. It comes from an indomitable will." **Mahatma Gandhi**

"Physical fitness can neither be achieved by wishful thinking nor outright purchase." **Joseph Pilates**

Tame the Turbulence

Workout Your Worry

S top the stress in your life before it stops you—nothing you're worrying about is worth dying over. Right? I realize this statement is far easier said than done. However, there is no denying that it is true. So what are we to do?

Maneuver number six, *workout your worry,* helps *tame the turbulence* in both our heads and our hearts. Choosing to incorporate exercise into our lives can help alleviate a great degree of stress, while also getting our bodies in better physical shape. Doing so consistently, though, usually means altering our view about working out.

It is wonderful to see that our society has become more health-conscious, with an increased focus on the importance of exercise. Yet, just because we know we should do it doesn't mean we will heed the advice. According to a 2012 Gallup poll, a slim majority of Americans exercise frequently, while nearly half do not, including 29.7 percent who reported not exercising for thirty minutes on any day in the past week. My guess is that those same individuals have not exercised well beyond just last week. Because once an exercise routine is on stand-by, it can be really tough to get back to following a steady flight plan.

I know this occurs because I have experienced times like this in my life. It is important to realize that, even though we may have gaps in our exercise regime, it is really important to get back to working out just as soon as we can.

According to the American Heart Association, lack of exercise drastically increases the risk of heart problems— specifically coronary artery disease. But, by engaging in regular exercise, we can decrease our risk factors for high blood pressure, cholesterol, obesity and diabetes. The AHA advises us to get about thirty minutes of exercise *most* days of the week, at a moderate intensity level, and then harder when we've built up our stamina. This doesn't mean that you need to do a super strenuous exercise like running. They suggest activities like walking, biking, swimming, etc.

Understanding the numerous health benefits exercising brings and knowing that all we really have to do is walk, we *should* be able get on and stay on a regular exercise plan, right? As many likely know, it is much harder than it sounds.

It is true that working out can make your muscles ache and leave you exhausted instead of feeling energetic. It can even create anxiety thinking about it, as we attempt to squeeze in yet another thing to do. But why is the emotion many people feel about exercise one that screams, "Ugh!"? I think the answer for many of us resides in our perception about working out.

If you randomly asked 100 people if they want to be healthy, probably most or all of them would say, "Yes." If you asked those same individuals if they felt that exercising contributes to better health, likely most or all of them again would say, "Yes." The inner conflict, though, is based on the perception that working out produces an immediate *positive* result.

As mentioned earlier, starting a new exercise routine can cause less-than-desirable short-term outcomes like physical pain and anxiety, at least until we adapt to the new regimen. The benefits of enduring this pain are not clearly apparent nor are they immediate—hence the reason for our procrastination, avoidance, excuses, etc. However, isn't it possible to look beyond the initial misery and understand that if we want to attain and/or preserve a healthy mind and body, this physical and mental state is *earned*, with exercise being absolutely essential?

I recommend replacing any negative excuses that enter our mind with positive reasons about *why* we choose to workout. Altering our thoughts in a way that describes *why* we value taking care of ourselves is really helpful. After all…you *are* worth it!

So what are some of the benefits of exercise, both short- and long-term?

The most obvious one is that working out helps slash our stress—once again, the number one health issue of the 21st Century. It does so by providing an effective outlet for frustrations. When life's annoyances build up, we need a safe way to release anger, irritation or aggravation. Exercise also helps ease our stress by helping to take our minds off of problems. I'm not suggesting you should avoid thinking about issues; rather, I am saying that exercise can help you temporarily redirect your focus.

Even though exercise truly can help us *avoid losing it, and fly through it,* that may not be reason enough for some. If you want or need additional motivation, here are a few more positive reasons from health experts as to why it's important to be physically active on a consistent basis:

- **Mood enhancer—you feel good!** Exercise is known to decrease "stress hormones" like cortisol and increase endorphins, which are your body's "feel-good" chemicals, giving your mood a natural boost.
- **Better sleep.** If you have difficulty sleeping, daily exercise can help. The more active your body is during the day, the more likely you are to relax fully at night and fall asleep easily. The idea is to give your body enough stimulation during the day, so you are not restless at night.
- **Enhanced sex life.** Physical improvements in muscle strength and tone, endurance, body composition, and cardiovascular function enhance sexual function in both men and women.
- **Weight control.** Regular exercise burns calories, increases metabolism, and helps to reach and maintain a healthy weight.

- **Enhanced physical appearance.** Working out helps us look more attractive in either a tight, sexy black dress or butt-hugging jeans.
- **Improved cognition and memory.** Exercise is known to stimulate the formation of new brain cells, namely in the areas of memory and learning. For example, older adults who engage in regular physical activity perform better in decision making, memory recall, and problem solving.
- **Positively influences blood pressure and cholesterol levels.** According to experts, exercise lowers blood pressure and favorably influences blood cholesterol levels by decreasing LDL (bad) cholesterol, triglycerides and total cholesterol, and increasing HDL (good) cholesterol.
- **Improved cardiovascular health.** Regular exercise makes your heart stronger—and a stronger heart pumps more blood with less effort.
- **Better muscle and bone strength.** Strength training increases muscle strength and mass, and decreases fat tissue. An active lifestyle also helps protect against osteoporosis, a disease that causes the bones to become weak and brittle.
- **Longevity.** People who are physically active usually live longer. According to numerous studies, regular exercise reduces the risk of premature death.

As you begin to *tame the turbulence* with exercise, you'll realize how working out can enhance the quality of your life.

The type of physical activity you engage in is a personal choice with numerous options available, such as:

- **Exercise classes**—aerobics, step aerobics, Zumba®, P90X®, water aerobics
- **Strength building**—Pilates, yoga, T'ai Chi, core training
- **Circuit training**—beginner weights, body-toning, weight training
- **Cardiovascular machines**—treadmill, elliptical, stepper, rower, bike
- **Team sports**—basketball, football, baseball, hockey, soccer, volleyball
- **Martial arts**—Karate, Tae kwon do, Ju Jitsu, kickboxing, mixed martial arts

I do realize that many of the above-mentioned activities require a fee to participate. Many of us, in these tough economic times, can't swing another payment. If money is a barrier, start a fitness routine at home…challenging yourself for free.

According to Pete McCall, an Exercise Physiologist with the American Council on Exercise, your own body weight and gravity can help both men and women get into great shape at home. For example, if you want to burn fat quickly, McCall says that rapid-fire circuits turn strength moves into calorie-torching, cardio work. A circuit may include push-ups, pull-ups and crunches, followed by a two-minute run around the room or in place. Repeat or alternate with a different circuit including bicep curls, dips, and shoulder presses to target smaller muscles.

If you don't own dumbbells or resistance bands and prefer not to purchase such equipment, use your creativity and have some fun looking around your living space for other items you could use. If you have a staircase in your home or apartment, going up and down those numerous times is a great way to feel your muscles burn, too, without any equipment needed.

Our bodies are made to move. As you aspire to *tame the turbulence* in your life, this key maneuver illustrates that by viewing exercise from a positive perspective along with engaging in consistent physical activity, the less tension you'll have. So, slide on your gym shoes and secure the laces. Who knows, you may meet some amazing new friends in the process. At a minimum, you'll increase your endorphins, enhance your health and wellbeing, and *workout your worry*.

Chapter 7

Make it a Fundae!

*"We don't stop playing because we turn old, but turn old because we stop playing." **Unknown***

*"The doors we open and close each day decide the lives we live." **Flora Whittemore***

*"The best vitamin to be a happy person is B_1." **Unknown***

Tame the Turbulence

Make it a Fundae!

When was the last time your belly hurt so bad from hysterically losing it through laughter? For some of us, we may not be able to recall. It's been reported that four-old kids laugh upwards of about 400 times a day. For adults, the number is far less. We are on record of averaging somewhere in the low teens. When does the world change from being fantastically funny to super serious?

As we grow up, from elementary school through middle school and into high school, we tend to be so concerned with what others think about us in terms of looks, fads, name brands, fitting in, having the latest gadget, etc. Then as we continue to age, do we become too old or *mature* to laugh at certain things that are truly funny?

If we want to *tame the turbulence* in our lives, one fairly easy maneuver is to experience more moments every day that are fun, inspiring and joyful. At times, I realize that some may need to search really hard for levity hidden in the weeds, yet I do believe that our lives are infused with so much goodness that we just need to notice and appreciate more of it.

Take, for instance, one of the very first jobs I had, proudly working at Ponderosa Steakhouse at the young age of 16. I recall many fond memories of my three years with them, but one in particular stands out like a flashing beacon.

It was a very busy day at the restaurant, and I was selected to be a "runner" on this particular shift, meaning I had to deliver the food to the customers—with each entrée platter consisting of a wooden base with a metal insert that kept the food hot. When the serving tray was at capacity, it held six entrees, which was quite heavy and difficult to manage.

It was about 12:30 p.m. and I had just finished serving one table, with another large order ready to go. I quickly placed each of the six platters on my tray and headed back to the dining area. I needed to grab some ketchup and steak sauce from the condiment station, located in the middle of the dining room. Because the condiment counter was higher than waist level, I had to hoist the tray up and use my torso to guide it onto the counter. This carefully calculated process also helped give my aching arms and shoulders a brief reprieve. My aim on this particular lift, however, was slightly off.

As I started to boost the tray up, I used a little too much force and the entire tray came toward me. Unable to react quickly enough, each platter, as if in slow motion as I tried to avoid the inevitable, crashed to the ceramic-tile floor, each of the six metal plates separating from its wooden base, clanging back and forth, faster and faster the lower it got to the floor.

The clangor went on for what seemed like an eternity, and then came silence—a long, uncomfortable stretch of silence. Next came a few whispers like, "Oh my goodness...can you imagine?" I paused, looked down at the mess, and flicked one left-over Salisbury steak that was still perched on my left shoulder, off and onto the floor next to the rubble that was intended to be a family's feast. A young girl I could see out of the corner of my eye began to giggle softly, and as the sound of her laughter grew, out came a powerful snort! I turned to her and started to laugh, too; and before we knew it, many patrons were joining in, as several even came over to help clean up the heap—including the father of the family's meal I had destroyed, who was unbelievably empathetic toward me.

Interestingly, in a matter of moments, my thoughts had transitioned from, "Should I run and hide?" to "Let's stop taking the situation quite so seriously." After all, no one got hurt; just some food ended up on the floor. Big deal. In forty-five minutes, all of the patrons who witnessed the act were gone, and the only people left to harass me were my co-workers. Trust me, they had plenty of their own moments of humiliation I could easily remind them of, if necessary.

What could have been a long, agonizing shift turned into a playful, light-hearted, and camaraderie-building "fundae," with my perspective changing instantly, all from a boisterous snort. I could've easily dwelled on the embarrassment I felt; however, I chose to focus on the moment as an opportunity to laugh at myself and fly through the turbulence.

Make it a Fundae!

Let's admit it, laughter and humor are infectious. In fact, that is what many people call my distinct laugh when I'm on a roll. The sound of roaring laughter is far more contagious than any cough, sniffle or sneeze. When shared, laughter brings people together and fills the room with happiness and warmth. Laughter also triggers healthy physical changes in the body. It boosts energy, diminishes pain, and protects you from the damaging effects of stress. Best of all, this priceless medicine is fun, free and easily accessed.

According to a June 2012 article published on www.helpguide.org entitled, "Laughter is the Best Medicine: The Health Benefits of Humor and Laughter," laughter brings incredible benefits to your life, including lightening your burdens, inspiring hopes, connecting you to others, and keeping you more grounded, focused and alert. They went on to share additional advantages, including:

- **Laughter relaxes the whole body.** A good, hearty laugh relieves physical tension and stress, leaving your muscles relaxed for up to forty-five minutes.
- **Laughter boosts the immune system.** Laughter decreases stress hormones and increases immune cells and infection-fighting antibodies, thus improving your resistance to disease.
- **Laughter triggers the release of endorphins.** The natural act of laughing increases endorphins, which are chemicals in the brain that promote an overall sense of well-being.

- **Laughter protects the heart.** Laughter improves the function of blood vessels and increases blood flow, which can help protect you against a heart attack and other cardiovascular problems.
- **Laughter dissolves distressing emotions.** You can't feel anxious, angry or sad when you're laughing.
- **Laughter helps you relax and recharge.** It reduces stress and increases energy, enabling you to stay focused and accomplish more.
- **Humor shifts perspective.** It allows you to see situations in a more realistic, less threatening light. A humorous perspective creates psychological distance, which can help you avoid feeling overwhelmed.

If you want to *tame the turbulence* in your life, one maneuver to try is allowing yourself to experience more precious moments every day that fill you with joy, humor and inspiration. Don't let those magical moments fly by. Choose to notice and appreciate them. A few examples include: Hearing my sons crack up over a side-splitting video on YouTube; or me tripping over a power cord after presenting to a group and losing all power to the room— oops!; or walking in the kitchen to find my dog feverishly devouring a tiered cupcake tower I was planning to surprise my husband with for his birthday; or in the midst of our family eating Thanksgiving dinner my youngest son says, "Mom, today I found Snickers (our dog) licking this turkey on the floor—but don't worry, I picked it up and put it back on the plate to finish thawing out." Decide to laugh a little more and let the tension go. Choose to make today a fundae!

Chapter 8

Poise Over Pressure

"No one can make you feel inferior without your consent." **Eleanor Roosevelt**

"It took me a long time not to judge myself through someone else's eyes." **Sally Field**

"Wherever you go, no matter what the weather, always bring your own sunshine." **Anthony J. D'Angelo**

Tame the Turbulence

Poise Over Pressure

People often share personal stories about struggling with self-confidence—an issue that many battle with their entire lives. Am I smart enough? Am I tall enough? Am I pretty or handsome enough? Am I experienced enough? Am I talented enough? Am I good enough?

Diminished self-confidence not only affects how you perceive yourself, it also has an enormous impact on how others view you. If you lack the self-confidence you desire, that turbulence may be standing in the way of you and the success you dream about. Instead, practice *poise over pressure*. Employing this maneuver will enhance your self-confidence steadily, ultimately removing this stressor from your life.

Self-confidence is about believing in you. When you look in the mirror, how do you rate yourself on a 10-point self-esteem scale? If you think you are a smokin' hot 15, you may need a reality check. If you rate yourself beneath a five, you likely will never live up to your potential and are doomed a failure. Right? Wrong! Self-confidence has nothing to do with *what* you see in the mirror. It is about *who* you see in the reflection.

Who really cares what your number is anyway, and I mean that at every level—whether I am referring to the scale, measuring tape, IQ score, GPA, or performance rating. Now, I realize these numbers have value, yet I don't believe we should determine our self-worth based on those figures. We are more than just numbers. Heck, I used to determine the type of day I was going to have by what number glared back at me every morning I timidly stepped on the square white box that would seal my fate for the next twenty-four hours. Not cool. We are definitely more than any number we or others assign.

What I have come to find is there simply is nothing more appealing than talking with or observing an individual with a strong sense of self-confidence. It is attractive to see individuals who feel good about themselves and who radiate that they are comfortable in their own skin; each with who they are as a person. These types of individuals also seem to be more in control of their emotions and able to work through stress with greater strength and determination.

If you long for greater poise and self-confidence, there are ways you can build it. Sometimes we need a little help getting the ideas flowing to lead us in the right direction. Below is a list of ten suggestions to take you down the path to stunning self-confidence. Select a few that sound interesting or appeal to your individual style. If they work...awesome! If they don't, try a few others. Here they are, in no particular order:

1. **Look your best**. If you are running errands, going to work, or meeting a friend/client for lunch, you'll feel better when you look great. If you are used to slacks and a shirt/blouse, dress it up with a fashionable piece of jewelry or a new belt. If you wear traditional suits, add a new scarf or tie to take it up a notch. Instead of wearing the comfortable outfit, pull out the classy one that looks sharp and leaves you feeling amazing.

2. **Smile**. In addition to your clothes, wear a smile. It's easy and helpful. You'll appear warm, friendly, and more approachable when you offer a genuine smile. You'll be able to influence others with less difficulty and they will feel more inclined to trust you, help you and listen to you, too. Yet, when you don't smile, your self-confidence is impacted, and those you're communicating with will notice, as well. Smiling is simple, effective and reaps big rewards.

3. **Don't allow people to take their frustrations out on you.** A colleague of mine refuses to sit back and take it when someone yells and screams at her over issues at work. She calmly yet assertively says, "I don't get combat pay; we can talk when you settle down."

4. **Hang around fun, inspiring people**. Avoid the Debbie Downers and Pessimistic Pauls. Hang out with more positive influences, like Motivating Michaels or Enthusiastic Ellens. You will become who you choose to spend time with. Instead of the energy deplete, connect with those who help you feel complete.

5. **Avoid making it your problem**. Sometimes we want to help others with an issue they share with us, and it makes a lot of sense to do so. Providing helpful and trusted quality guidance is what being a great friend or confidant is about. Yet other situations are better handled by listening, expressing empathy, and then carefully suggesting another source to help him/her, like a professional with expertise in that area. Be careful not to take on and own the problems of others. Instead, allow them to be responsible for their own actions, thoughts and feelings.

6. **Write in a journal**. Take a few minutes each day to channel your thoughts and write several of them in a special place. Maybe it is a journal focused on those things that bring you joy, or people you are grateful for, or ways in which you are overcoming a fear. Whatever warrants repetitive thought deserves to be written down. Journaling gives you a way to remind yourself of people you appreciate, things you are thankful for, and progress you have made.

7. **Write ten things you are good at or qualities you like in yourself.** Carry a list of your positive traits with you at all times, so they are close and ready to be referenced. If a negative thought enters your mind or someone makes a comment that is tough to overcome quickly, pull out your list of positive attributes or strengths and remind yourself of your gifts and talents. A simple affirmation helps put things back into perspective.

8. Prepare. I feel most confident when I am prepared. I feel far more anxious and uncertain when I am unprepared. Whatever task or initiative you are focused on, be sure you put your heart and soul into it, and come prepared. As my husband always says, "Preparation is where planning meets opportunity." When you are prepared, you can fly through unforeseen turbulence, as if on auto-pilot.

9. Arrive early. One thing I have learned the hard way is that arriving late is good for no one. And this point relates to any meeting, appointment or engagement you can think of. The person who is awaiting your arrival is often worried and nervous about why you are late or if you are still coming. You, the late individual, are likely racing down the streets or highway, trying to make up for lost time. Instead, plan to arrive early and give yourself a few minutes to gather your thoughts, use the restroom, and demonstrate that you value the person's time you are meeting with. If you arrive earlier than expected and the other person is still tied up, bring along something to occupy your time productively, such as: Listening to an audio CD, catching up on some reading, reviewing documents that need your attention, or returning a phone call.

10. Set one small goal and achieve it. Nothing breeds success more than success itself. Identify one small, yet important goal that you would like to attain. Understand clearly what needs to happen to accomplish that goal. Put it in writing and ensure you keep that goal front and center, reminding yourself about it daily. Once you achieve it, celebrate in an appropriate way, relative to the size and meaning of the goal. By accomplishing small goals, you create momentum that will perpetuate and gain traction. Your self-confidence will be at a well-deserved high, which will provide even more assurance that you can attain what you set out to do next.

Like a thief in the night, stress can rob your self-confidence. Don't let it! Apply tips from this maneuver to *tame the turbulence*. Choose *poise over pressure*, so when you look in the mirror, you'll see the reflection you desire and deserve.

Chapter 9

Reflections Become Reality

"It's so hard when I have to, and so easy when I want to." **Annie Gottlier**

"Being in a good frame of mind helps keep one in the picture of health." **Unknown**

"The best things in life are yours if you can appreciate them." **Dale Carnegie**

Tame the Turbulence

Reflections Become Reality

It was Friday on a fall day years ago when I signed the mortgage papers for a brand new, three-bedroom ranch-style house that was built just for me. As a single woman, I was told repeatedly that I didn't want to go through something like this alone, but I was certain I really did. How is it that some feel they know what is best for you?

As I unlocked the door to my new home, it was the most amazing feeling ever. My decisions were reflected in the architecture, floor-plan, lighting, tile, carpet, fireplace, molding, counter tops, cabinets, hardware, and so on. All of my hard work selecting what I wanted to have in *my* house, appeared in front of me. Soon the appliances were delivered, and then the movers arrived, taking most of my belongings into the basement, so I could arrange them as time and energy permitted.

This day was so exciting! After all, owning a home is the American dream. I proudly reached a milestone that many wish for, and felt humbled and truly blessed.

After a long, exhausting and emotional day, I finally ran out of oomph and retired to my comfy bed, which felt so good to my aching muscles. I slept soundly and got up to work another lengthy, fatiguing day. As I crawled into bed on night number two, it began to rain. As the storm moved through, I woke several times from loud thunder and lightning, and rose Sunday morning about 6:00 a.m. to begin a third day of unpacking.

Looking for a specific item and realizing it was stored among most of my belongings still in the basement, I turned the light on and headed down the steps. As I made it about halfway, I gasped! My basement was filled with 6 inches of water, a steady stream still flowing in through one of the small windows. Overcome with disbelief and despair, I sat down on one of the steps and added a bucket of tears to the already over-worked sump pump.

Having relieved some of the intense emotion, it was time to brush away the tears and take action. I placed four phone calls: One to my friend who drove right over; the next to the builder, where I left a message; the third to a restoration crew who said they would be there within an hour; and my last call was to the realtor.

My friend, Sara, arrived with two pair of rain boots, and we proceeded down the stairs to reveal the devastation and try to reclaim what we could. Following her down the steps, it was like the next minute happened in slow motion. As she stepped off the last dry step and put one foot into the murky water, she glanced up and noticed an electrical outlet on the wall with a dehumidifier plugged into it as her other foot now also entered the water. Without hesitation, she spun back around and retracted her steps as quickly as possible, screaming, "Oh my God...the breaker!"

It was an absolute miracle that Sara wasn't electrocuted. The breaker must have switched off all current to the basement, with the lights being on a different circuit. We knew how lucky we were; how quickly our lives could have been so different. Everything after that pivotal moment was immediately put in perspective. That's not to say working through the ordeal was easy to deal with, but it certainly was easier than it could have been.

The restoration crew arrived, and I began to scoop out floating pictures, hand-made keepsakes, and precious mementos, being overtaken with sadness and loss. My dream turned into a nightmare in less than 48 hours.

It was determined that the sump pump was hooked up incorrectly, with the water flowing back into the window-well, instead of into the street. The crews also were behind a bit and hadn't finished back-filling the dirt up to the edge of the house. But because they didn't want to delay the closing of my loan, which turned the ownership over to me and allowed me to move in as scheduled, they promised they would return Monday morning to finish the job. The lack of backfill acted as a moat for the heavy rains to accumulate, which made for the perfect storm. Moreover, even though I had sump pump coverage, I didn't have flood insurance, which is what this situation demanded.

Finally after weeks of enormous suction hoses, commercial-grade fans, construction crews, cleaning teams, and endless hours of drudgery, my house was back to a *new* normal. The fresh, new smell had vanished, replaced by a damp aroma that diminished with time. Nonetheless, the ordeal was over, thankfully with the builder paying most of the expense.

In dealing with unforeseen turbulence, how do you turn your thoughts from a victim mentality, with feelings of anger and hopelessness, to something completely different? Yes, there is no question I felt tremendously grateful that Sara wasn't injured or worse. Yet, how did I overcome the disorder and chaos that kept running through my mind and fly through it?

First, I knew that my thoughts and attitude determine the path and ultimately the outcome of my life. Did I want to continue to live this nightmare, or would I rather move through this pain as quickly as possible and get back to living my dream? The choice was obvious; once I embraced it emotionally, the rest of me followed.

I am a strong believer in affirmative self-talk. I think it paves the way for a positive, successful and meaningful life. It shapes our moment-to-moment thoughts and influences our choices, greatly impacting events and outcomes.

Let's say I wake up on a Saturday morning and these are the words I use: "Today I need to drop the kids off at basketball practice by 9:00 a.m. and then pick up a prescription from the pharmacy. Next, I have to run to get a few things from the grocery store, and then I need to make a quick stop at the bank. After that, my dry-cleaning must get picked up, and I need to hurry back to the gym to get the boys by 11:00 a.m."

What I've just done in this example is use demanding statements on myself, which opens up a lot of opportunities to say irrational things. This behavior creates a highly stressful situation—not only for me, but for those loved ones hanging out with me, plus anyone who comes into contact with me. Would you like to spend a Saturday morning like this with me? I wouldn't want to spend it with myself.

When you use demanding statements, you create turbulence in your head; a scenario of "what ifs" that sounds like, "What if I don't get this done?" or "What if I don't get there in time?" or "What if this?" or "What if that?" This is when you really begin to lose it and spiral wildly out of control. Can you relate?

What I recommend to *tame this turbulence* is to stop the vicious cycle of negative self-talk. Acknowledge when you hear yourself say either aloud or in your head, "have-to," "must," or "need-to" statements. Then replace the needs, musts and haves with preferences, desires and wants, stating "want to" or "would like to" instead.

What if you don't pick up the prescription today? What if you don't make it to the bank? What if you're late picking up the kids? It's not what you wanted, it may even lead to some consequences, but in the overall scheme of things, you likely can live with it just fine. Reframe negative self-talk instead of accepting it.

In addition to replacing some of the language we use, we can also enhance our self-talk in other ways. Here are a few terrific tips just for you:

- **Wake up fifteen minutes earlier.** Have this extra time available, so that if something unexpected happens, you don't have to feel or be rushed.
- **Go to the grocery store before work and buy a bouquet of fresh flowers.** Put the flowers in a glass of water and smell them often.
- **Jam to your favorite songs.** Do this on the way to work and on the way home.
- **Take fifteen minutes to clean your desk or workstation.** This may mean putting piles of paperwork into file folders, tossing some stuff you don't really need, or grabbing some paper towel and a cleaning solvent. It is so nice to be in a clean and orderly space.
- **Take a nice colleague out to lunch.** Doing something unexpected for someone else always makes us feel wonderful.
- **Indulge in a sweet treat.** After you handled a particular task that you have either avoided or didn't

look forward to, reward yourself! Treat yourself to something you find pleasurable. Reward yourself right away because you deserve it.

- **Read a quick passage from my inspirational series, *Moments of Motivation*.** Open to any page and enjoy an uplifting and optimistic message created to bring a smile to your face throughout the day.

As Earl Nightingale said, "It's our attitude in life that determines life's attitude toward us." How true that statement is. If we view life through an optimistic lens, others will view us as positive and hopeful individuals. Likewise, our views and reactions, whether positive or negative, will become our reality. As this maneuver suggests, avoid negative distractions in our mind, because *reflections become reality*. Navigate your thoughts toward the positive alternative instead.

Chapter 10

Plan, Persevere and Prosper

"When you come to the end of your rope, tie a knot and hang on." **Franklin D. Roosevelt**

"Plan your work for today and every day—then work your plan." **Norman Vincent Peale**

"All of our dreams can come true—if we have the courage to pursue them." **Walt Disney**

Tame the Turbulence

Plan, Persevere and Prosper

Every New Year, people resolve to lose weight, stop smoking, eat healthier, save money, etc., etc. They start the New Year fresh, with great optimism that this year will be different; they *will* attain their goal.

However, according to a 15,000-respondent survey conducted by time management experts FranklinCovey, a full 35 percent of New Year's resolutions are broken before the end of January, dwindling to only 23 percent being honored. So why do so many people struggle with keeping a promise they made to a hopeful self?

Forty percent of those surveyed cited having too many things to do to keep their commitment. Another 35 percent said that not fulfilling their resolutions came down to not being committed to the resolutions they made in the first place.

Personally, I am not interested in setting New Year's resolutions. Why wait until January 1 to make a change I know needs attention now or set a goal I could have accomplished by then? I think annual resolutions are a way to engage in supported procrastination. If I proclaim that I will begin this endeavor at the beginning of the year, and it is in the middle of November, I am essentially off the hook until January, and the chances of anyone remembering my resolution are not very good.

I believe the secret to persevering through to prosperity lies in the plan we outline and how we choose to follow it. When we identify a challenging yet attainable goal that aligns with our values, we can believe confidently in the vision to accomplish it and the benefits we likely will realize from it. Then, when we separate the goal into specific, timely, actionable objectives and share our intentions with others, we can more easily commit to this plan and follow through on our promises.

Knowing what we want to do with our lives, working through any turbulence we encounter, and then focusing on choices that lead us to success, is the tenth key maneuver. Below is a five-step process to *plan, persevere and prosper*:

Step 1: Determine what your values are and choose to live by them. Conflict arises when we are living out of sync with our core values. Our value system should be the foundational principle behind how we live our lives. For example, if your number one value is family and your job requires you to work 65 hours a week, is it any wonder you feel unsettled, super stressed, and generally unhappy? When you're clear about what is important to you, it is easier to let go of things that don't fit or make changes to better align your life with what matters most to you.

Step 2: Identify *one* challenging goal you want to achieve. Identifying one goal that is realistic yet challenging allows you to stretch beyond what you know you can do and reach for something that is slightly out of reach. When you focus on one goal, versus three, you will be able to design a more clearly targeted plan to help you achieve this desired goal.

Step 3: Be clear about the benefits of attaining your goal. Understanding the benefits to a newly defined goal is critical to staying motivated and maintaining commitment. Some benefits may be to:

- Live with integrity and character.
- Define a clear path for ourselves and others.
- Take action instead of just wishing.
- Stay focused on priorities and limit distractions.
- Enhance self-image and self-confidence.
- Achieve greater awareness of areas to improve.
- Accept credit for successes and responsibility for failures.
- Increase motivation for future goals from past accomplishments.

Step 4: Outline timely, specific objectives to reach your goal. This plan should define specific objectives that support attaining your goal. Be sure to put this plan in writing, so you can refer back to it often, maybe even daily. As you achieve identified objectives, reward yourself accordingly.

For example, say your goal is to become more physically fit over the course of the next three months. Some specific objectives to help you reach your goal could be:

- Walk 20 minutes/day, three days/week, for three weeks.
- Walk 30 minutes/day, four days/week, for the next four weeks, incorporating a walk/run on one of the days.
- Walk two days/week and walk/run three-four days/week, each for 30 minutes/day. Continue this routine for five weeks and re-evaluate how to proceed.

Step 5: Seek support from a few individuals you trust who will encourage you to remain committed. Reach consensus with these individuals before beginning as to how often they can expect to receive an update from you and how they can best encourage you and/or help hold you accountable if needed.

Even the best-laid plans go awry. Sometimes you prepare well, yet realize significant obstacles along the way. That's okay, because being flexible and adapting to challenging situations allows you to remain agile, which is a useful skill professionally and personally.

It was mid-October several years ago, and my husband challenged me to find a balmy getaway-spot for a modest price. Because we planned to travel over a holiday, I knew this would be difficult, as prices are usually higher and resorts are often booked. However, I was optimistic I would plan a beautiful retreat.

I researched numerous options and secured a vacation package in Mexico, selecting a gorgeous resort and spa that included a long list of impressive amenities. Our anticipation grew as departure day drew closer. Finally, it was time to board the jet and head south to immerse ourselves in exquisite luxury—or so we thought.

As the cab driver opened our vehicle doors, we caught our first real glimpse of the resort, which definitely didn't resemble the gorgeous pictures on their Web site. I verified that we were at the right spot, and we were assured this was our hotel. As we walked into the lobby, the flashing neon lights were...*unique*, and it reeked of a strange aroma. Exchanging questioning looks, I thought surely our rooms would be immaculate and beautiful.

As we approached the door to our first-floor room, we noticed a large hole, about the size of my fist, located about where the security chain would be found on the other side of the door. We noted the large gap under the door, too, which made us think of sharing our room with creepy critters. We were still optimistic that the room would take our breath away. And that it did.

The furniture was beat up, the water in the bathroom sink was a strange color and had a funky smell, and when I looked at the shower, the glass door was so thickly covered in soap scum and green grime that I couldn't even see through it. As we approached the patio that had clearly been busted through, a sloppy attempt at a repair being quite obvious, the replacement patio door was three or so inches from the floor, incapable of being locked.

Now, I am someone who has stayed at some doozy hotels in my life, but I always knew what I was getting. The pictures have always matched my expectations, which matched reality. This experience was different, and, we quickly started referring to this hotel as the Wild, Wild Warlock.

A drink sounded like a good idea, as we sipped on very watered-down drinks at the bar, with several cockroaches scurrying past our feet. I paused, and with a rush of reality permeating my body, realized our intended vacation was not even close to what we were expecting. I felt bad, wishing we could wave a magic wand and instantly alter our situation.

Kirt and I decided that together we would persevere through this problem. We developed a plan to tackle this issue head on. We chose to first contact the booking agency we originally went through, but soon found out our cell phones didn't work at this hotel. Let's see, we were in a different country, we didn't speak the language, our comfortable means of communication was severed, our arranged transportation wouldn't be back for another week, we didn't have a lot of cash due to pre-paying for the vacation, and, while exhausted from a full day of travel, we didn't feel safe enough to shut our eyes. This was not an ideal situation—to say the least.

That evening, my husband and I pulled off an amazing feat! Kirt remembered the name of a resort we stayed at previously. We didn't know exactly how far it was from where we were, but with the help of a friendly operator, we were connected to that resort. They informed us they were three hours away, but another resort that was part of their chain was only thirty minutes away. The manager we spoke to was able to verify that they had rooms available at the other resort, and she provided us their telephone number. Providing we could somehow work out the financial aspect of our challenging situation, we knew we had a place where we could transition to. It was time to talk with the manager of the Wild, Wild Warlock.

To our surprise, the manager was wonderful to work with. He empathized and said he would issue a full refund, even helping us work through our third-party online booking company. He also arranged secure transportation to the other hotel, which we were also very thankful for. By handling this tough situation calmly, kindly and respectfully, the manager was more willing to help us. After all, it is always much easier to be reasonable when you're not being threatened or screamed at.

This scenario represents an example of where even well-planned situations can go wrong; but with a *revised* plan and strong perseverance, you can dramatically change your circumstances, rising above the turbulence and directing you toward greater prosperity. In this particular case, we were very fortunate—an extra few hundred dollars, and in a matter of hours as if by magic, we landed at a beautiful five-star opulent resort, which exceeded our *wild*est expectations.

If you want to *tame the turbulence* in your life and begin to walk down the path to greater prosperity, it all begins with *you*. You have the power to create a detailed plan, and when challenges confront you, as they likely will, decide to be steadfast. *Plan, persevere and prosper*. Instead of negatively reacting to turbulence you encounter, choose to fly through it by honoring the goals you set and the promises you made to yourself and others.

Closing Thoughts

Turbulence on an airplane can feel so big, primarily because you're traveling so fast. When it feels like the plane just dropped thousands of feet, it likely only hit a bump, barely registering on the cockpit instruments. Why? The best analogy is driving over speed bumps in an automobile. Hit one at 10 mph and you barely feel it. Hit one at 80 mph and your head will bounce off the roof of your car. Now imagine hitting it at 500 mph?

Stress in our lives can feel much like the 500 mph turbulence. Daunting, scary, and even impossible to move through. But rather than becoming one of the 40+ percent of adults who suffer from adverse health effects caused by stress, choose to *tame the turbulence*. Just as pilots do—stay calm, take control, and apply one of the 10 Maneuvers you're now familiar with. Simply put...*Avoid losing it. Fly through it.*

About the Author

+ + + + +

 As a sought-after keynote speaker, established author, and a results-focused consultant, Tracy Butz is known for engaging her audiences and empowering them with innovative concepts and tools to become architects of their own lives.

Tracy has more than 18 years of experience connecting with both large- and small-size audiences from a wide range of industries, including the U.S. Army, Plexus, Subway Restaurants, 4imprint, and Great Northern Corporation, to name a few. She is well known for her captivating and dynamic delivery, where audiences can be found sitting on the edge of their seats, laughing aloud, and brushing away tears as she masterfully recounts each story, aligned with a key point, an impactful meaning, and an enduring message. Tracy truly delivers the tools for today's world, propelling her audiences to live more productive, passionate and purposeful lives.

Tracy Butz
Think Impact Solutions, LLC
www.tracybutz.com
920-450-2118
tracy@tracybutz.com

How Can You Use This Book?

Motivate

Educate

Thank

Inspire

Promote

Connect

Why have a personalized version of *Tame the Turbulence*?

- Build personal bonds with customers, prospects, colleagues and employees.

- Develop a long-lasting reminder of your event, milestone or celebration.

- Provide a keepsake that inspires change in behavior and leads to an enhanced life.

- Deliver the ultimate thank you gift that remains on coffee tables and bookshelves.

- Create the "wow" factor!

Books are thoughtful gifts that provide a genuine sentiment other promotional items cannot express. They promote employee discussions and interaction, reinforce an event's meaning, and make a lasting impression. Gift this book to say thank you and show your people you care.

More Books Authored by Tracy

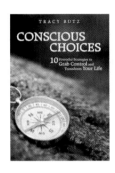

Conscious Choices: 10 Powerful Strategies to Grab Control and Transform Your Life

The Perfect Pair of Jeans: Design Your Life to Fit You Dream It. Plan It. Live It.

Monday's Motivational Message: Moments of Motivation Designed to Inspire

Books can be purchased at:
www.tracybutz.com